AUTO RACING

HUMOR

By
Charles S. Hellman and Robert A. Tiritilli

ISBN 0-935938-45-6
Illustrations by Robert A. Tiritilli
Cover & Interior Design by Charles S. Hellman
Edited by Charles S. Hellman

**"Listen pal,
you got the wrong PIT STOP!"**

Narrow minded race fans

This car, is car, a car, good car, way car, to car, keep car, a car, NASCAR car, idiot car, like car, you car, busy car, for car, 25 car, seconds car! Now read without the word car.

"I think we can save the helmet!"

"He never learned
how to make a LEFT turn!"

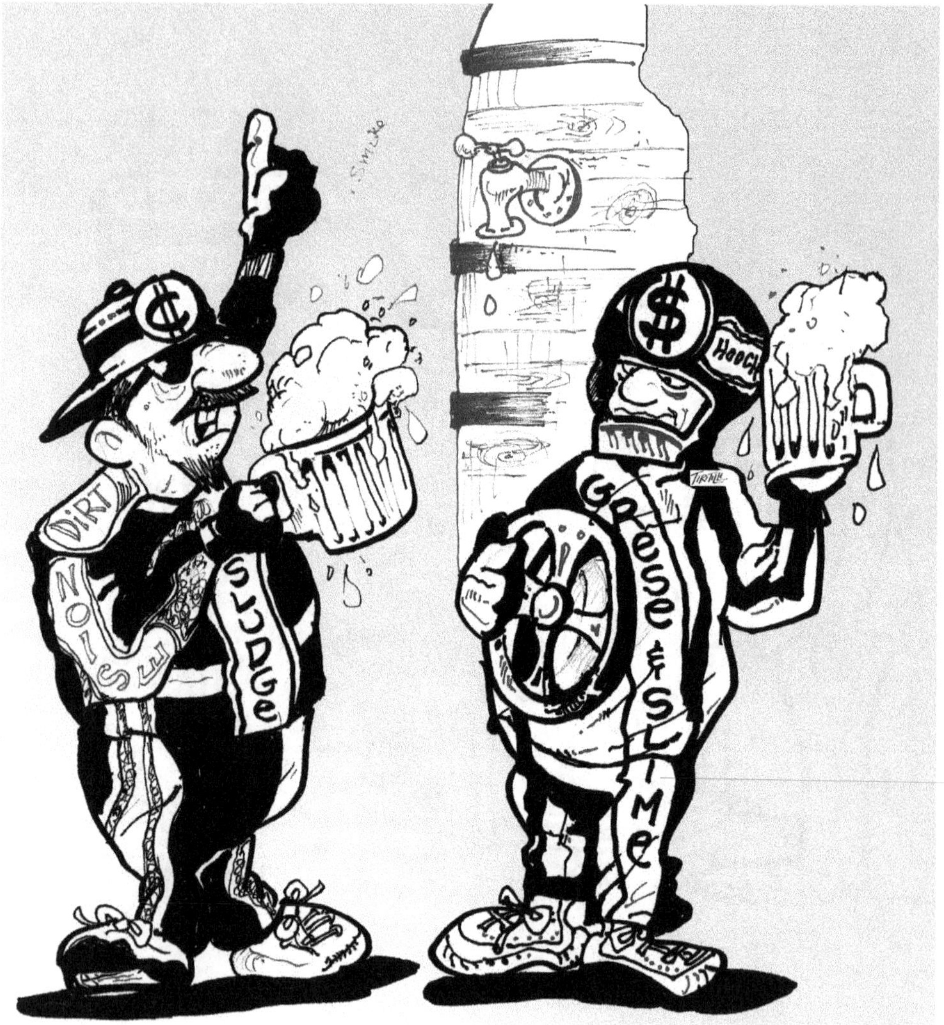
DiRT
NOISE
SLUDGE
GRESE & SLIME
Hooch

Now that's DRAFTING!

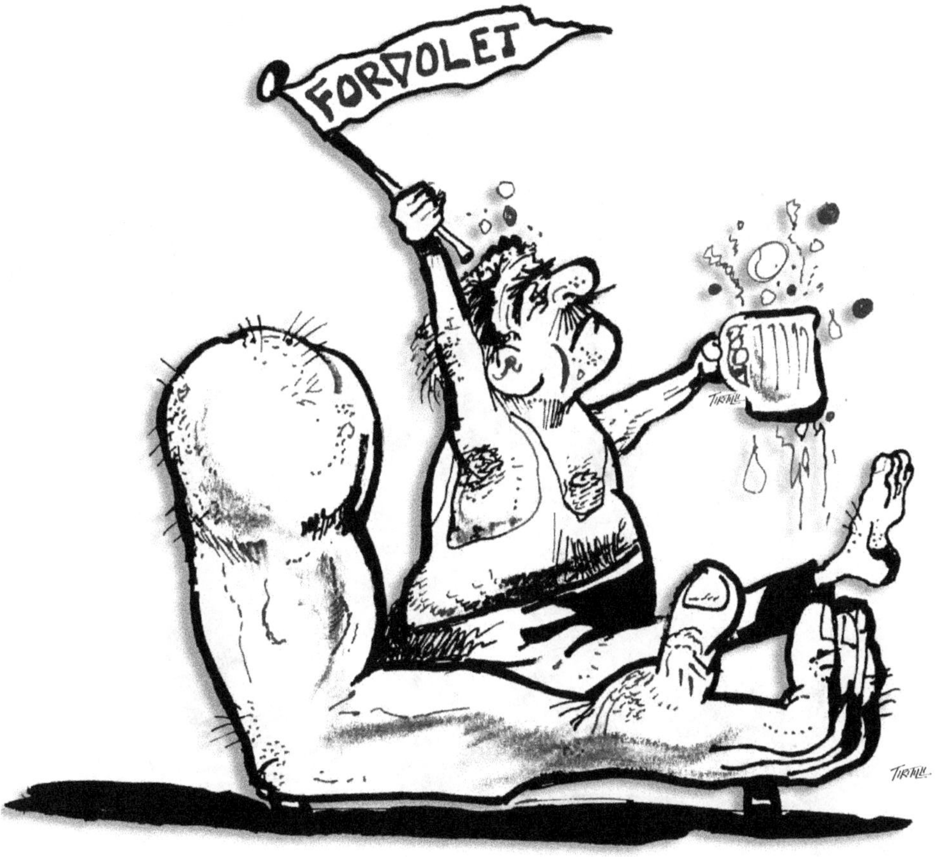
FORDOLET
TIRTALLI

Armchair race fan

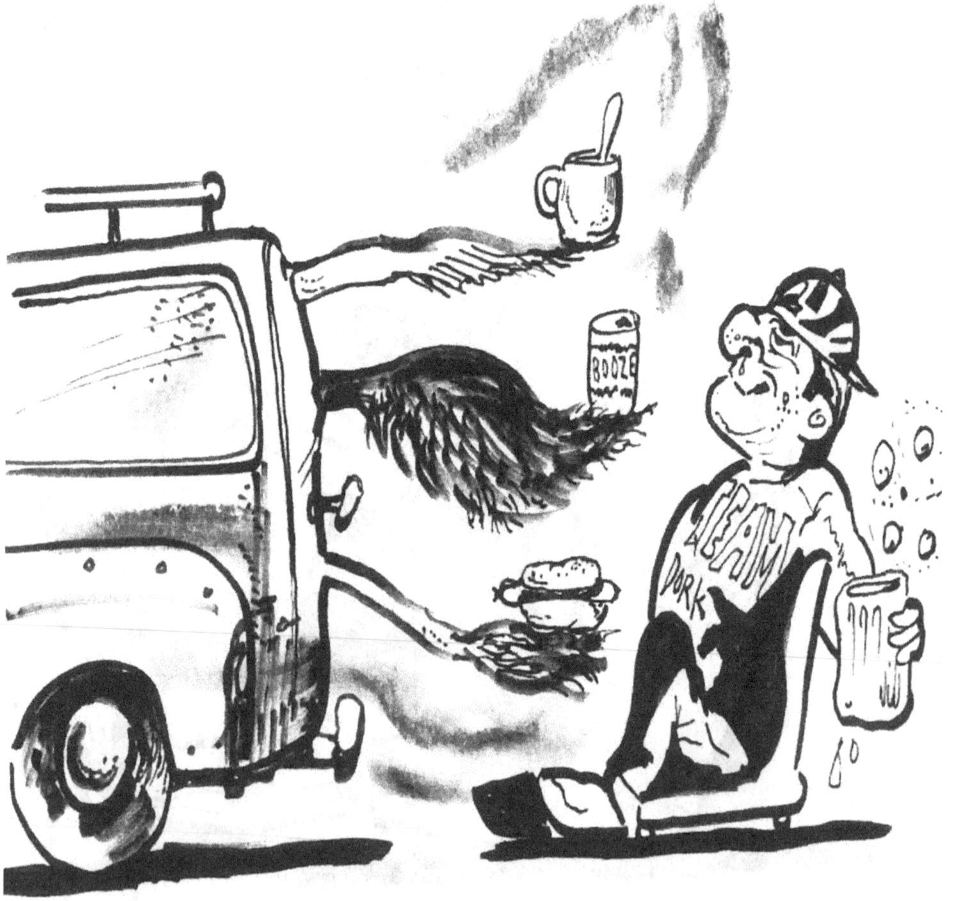
BOOZE
TEAM
DORK

Tailgate party

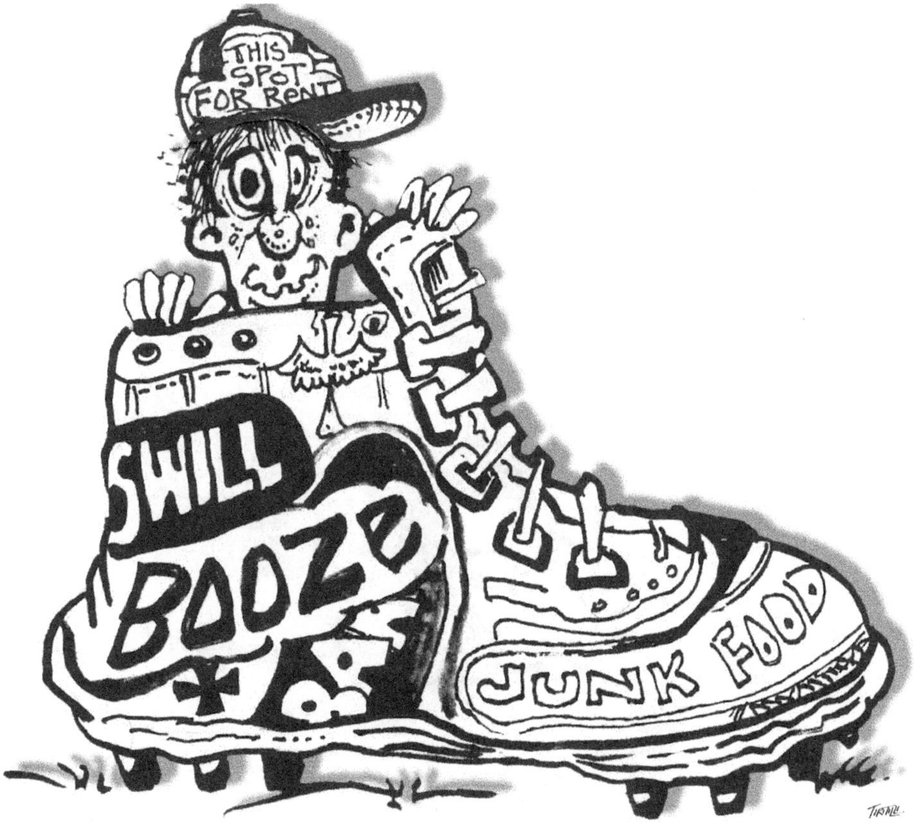
THIS SPOT FOR RENT
SWILL
BOOZE
JUNK FOOD

Something is "afoot"!

"They do add *class* to the race."

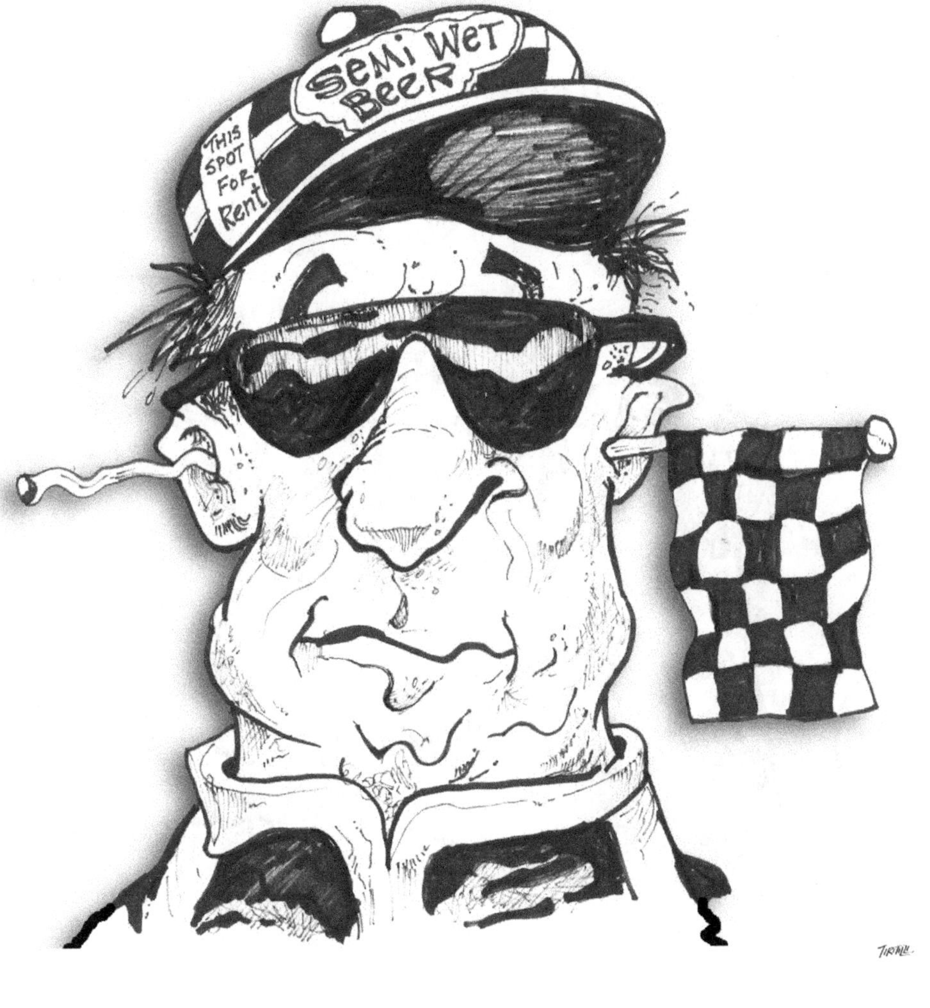
SEMI WET
BEER
THIS
SPOT
FOR
Rent

Auto-nomous

"Is it sponsored by Cleopatra?"

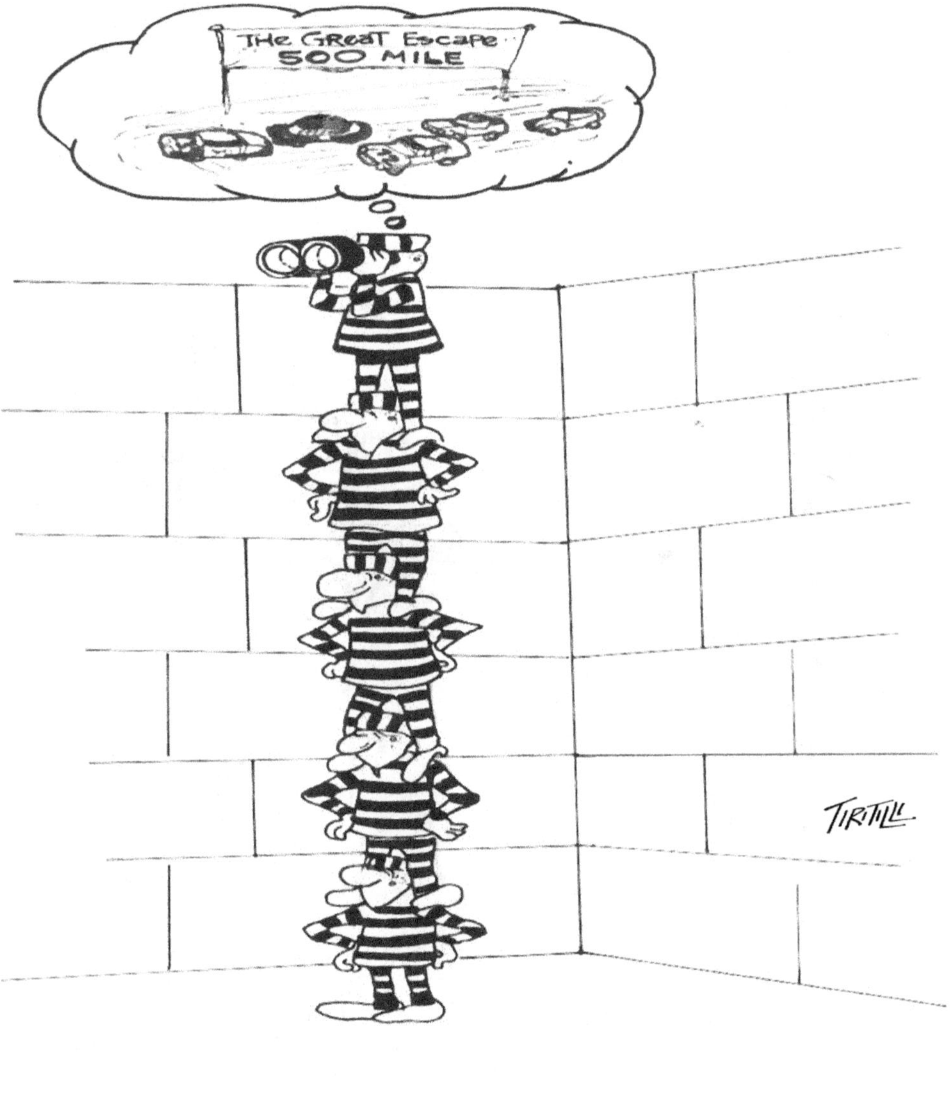
THE GREAT ESCAPE
500 MILE
TIRITILLI

**A new surgical way to get rid
of your spare tire!**

"Your favorite flag is the caution flag!"

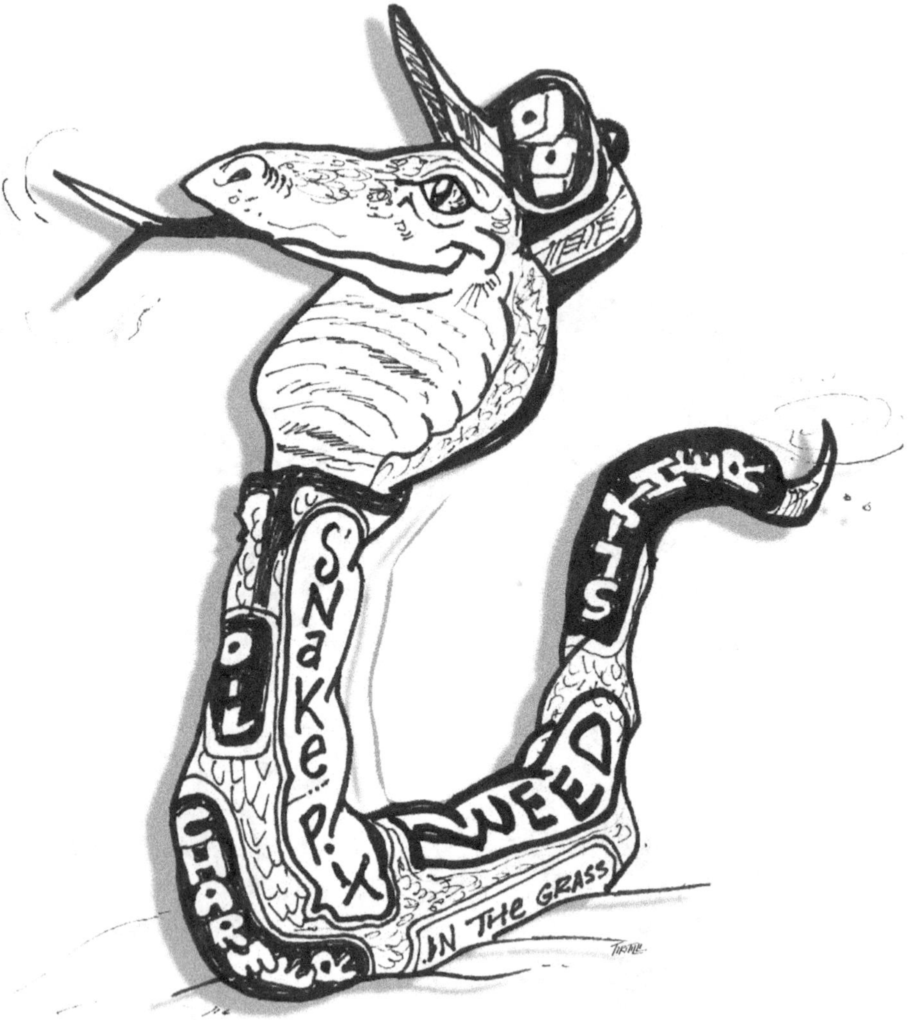
OIL
SNaKe
SLITHER
WEED
IN THE GRASS

Pit boss

"Are you sure this race car
can run on regular, unleaded gas?"

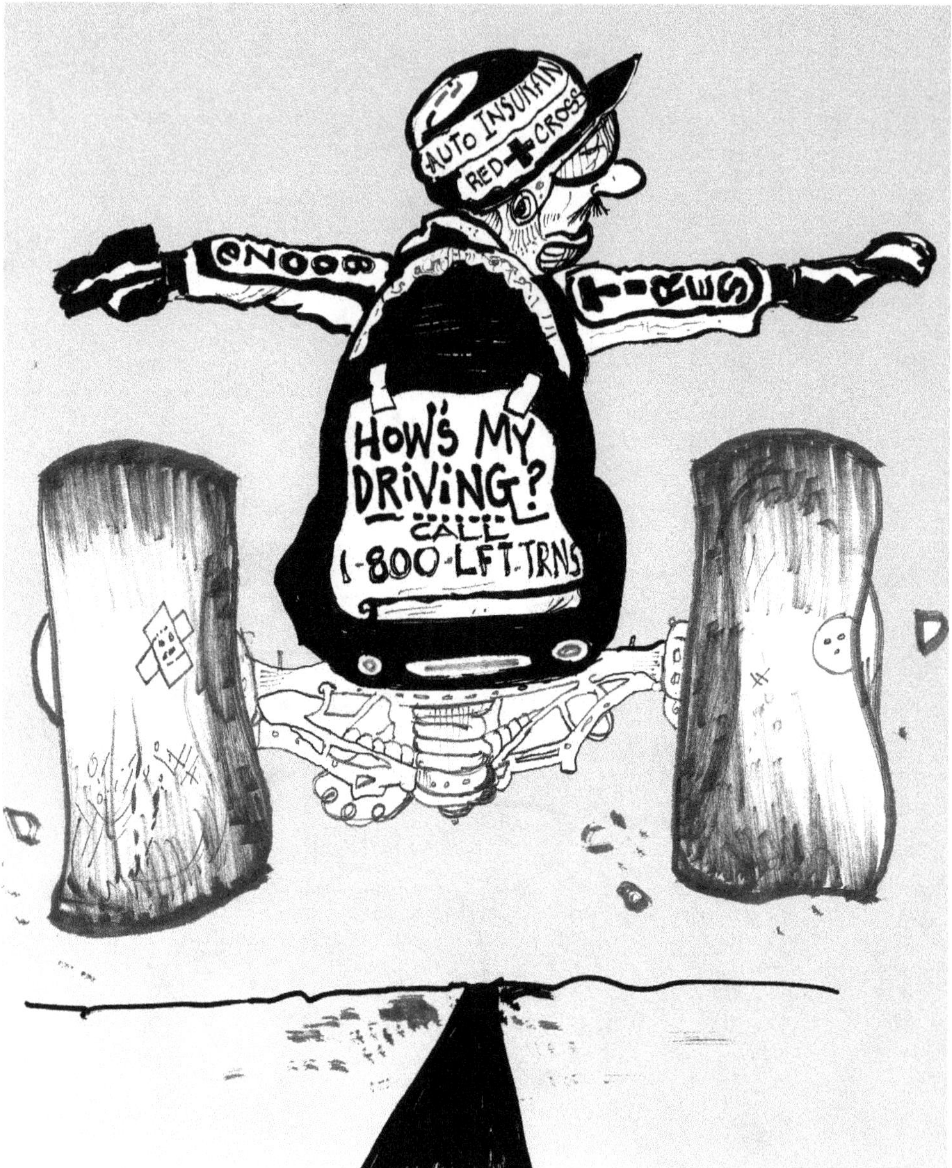
AUTO INSURAN
RED + CROSS
HOW'S MY DRIVING?
CALL
1-800-LFT-TRNS

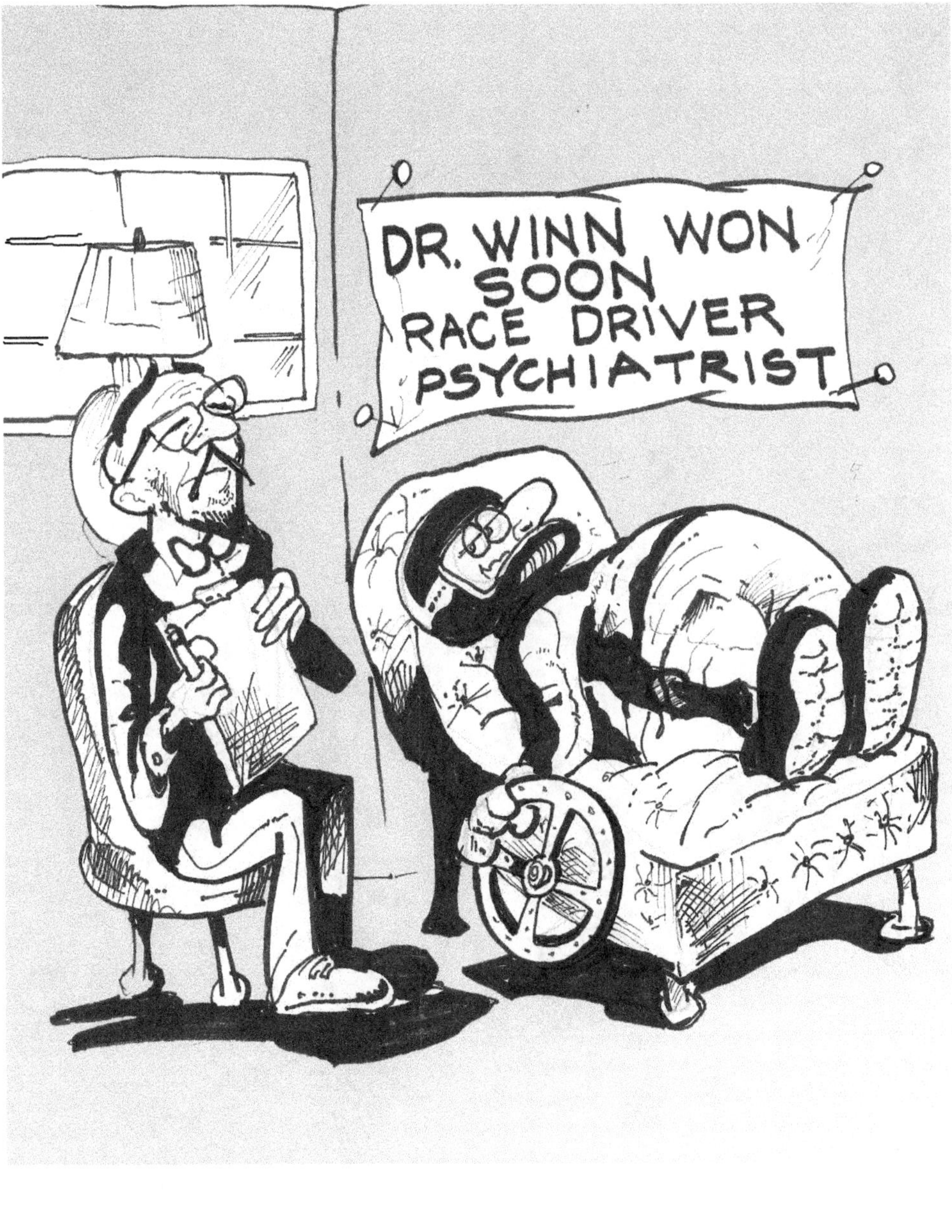
DR. WINN WON
SOON
RACE DRIVER
PSYCHIATRIST

"Dale *who* started this way?"

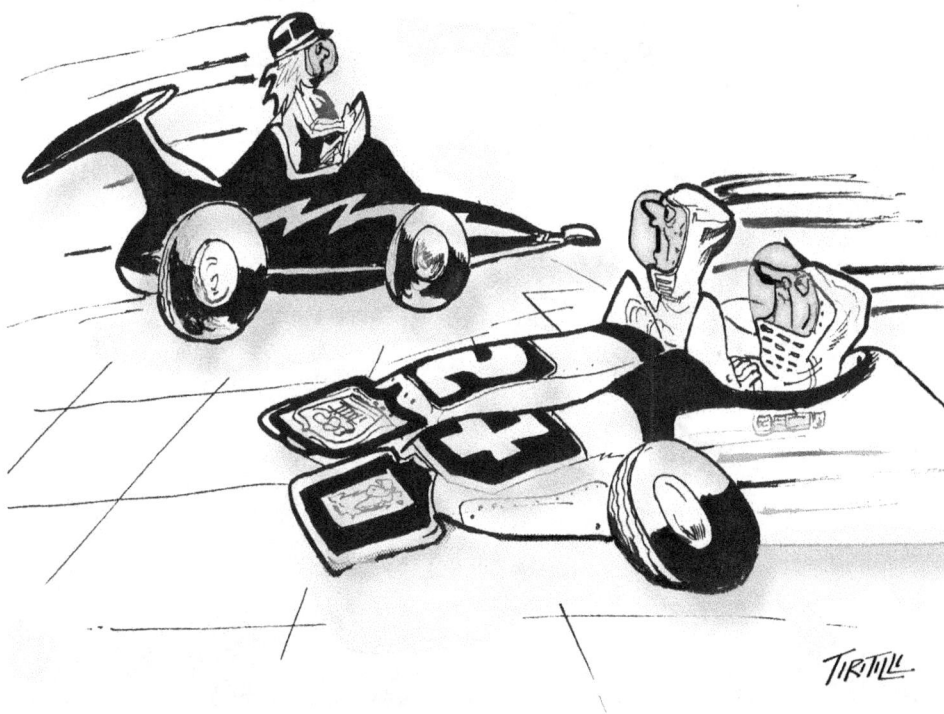

"See... she's done it again!"

"Professor, what kind of race car is it?"

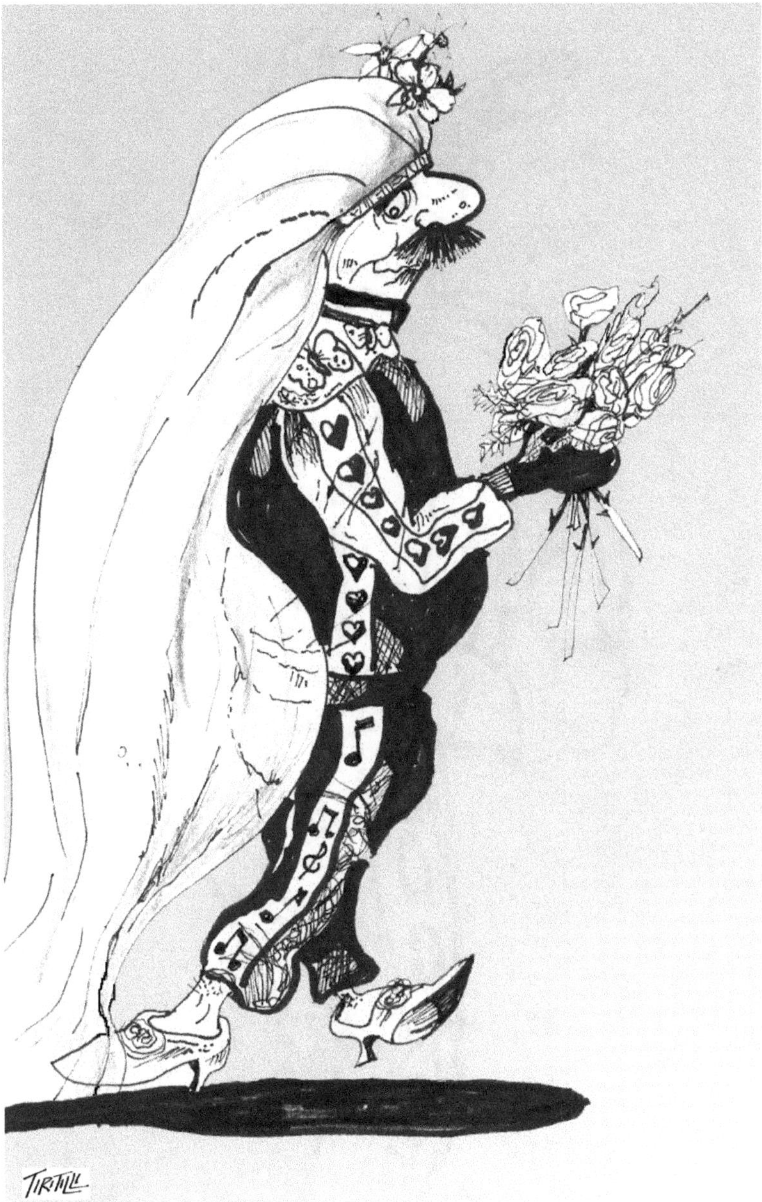
TIRITILLI

Drag Racer?

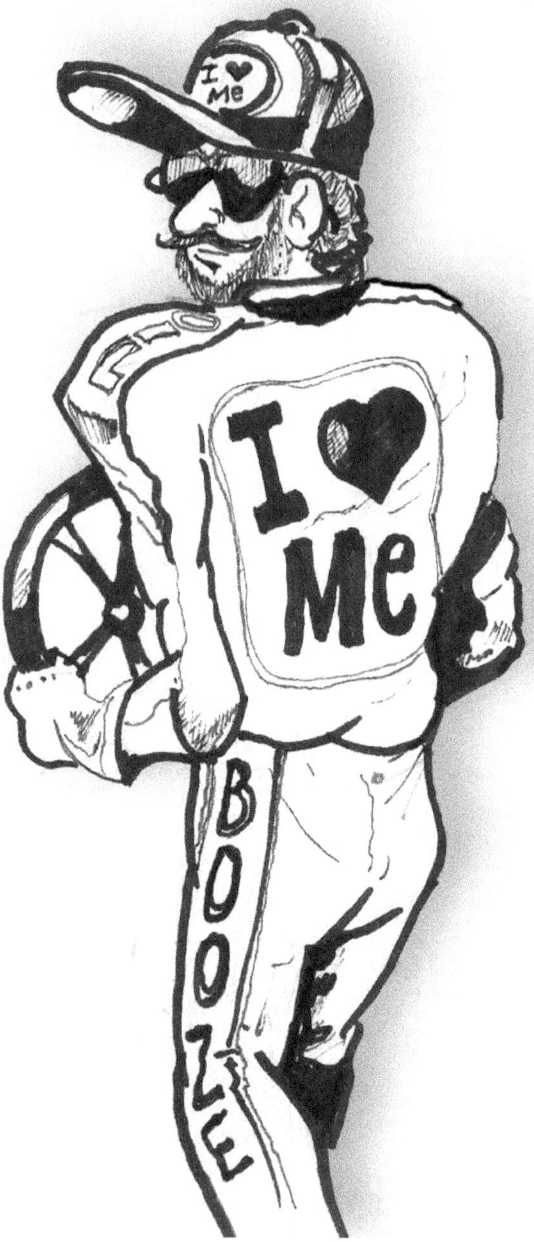
I ♥ Me
I ♥ Me
BOOZE

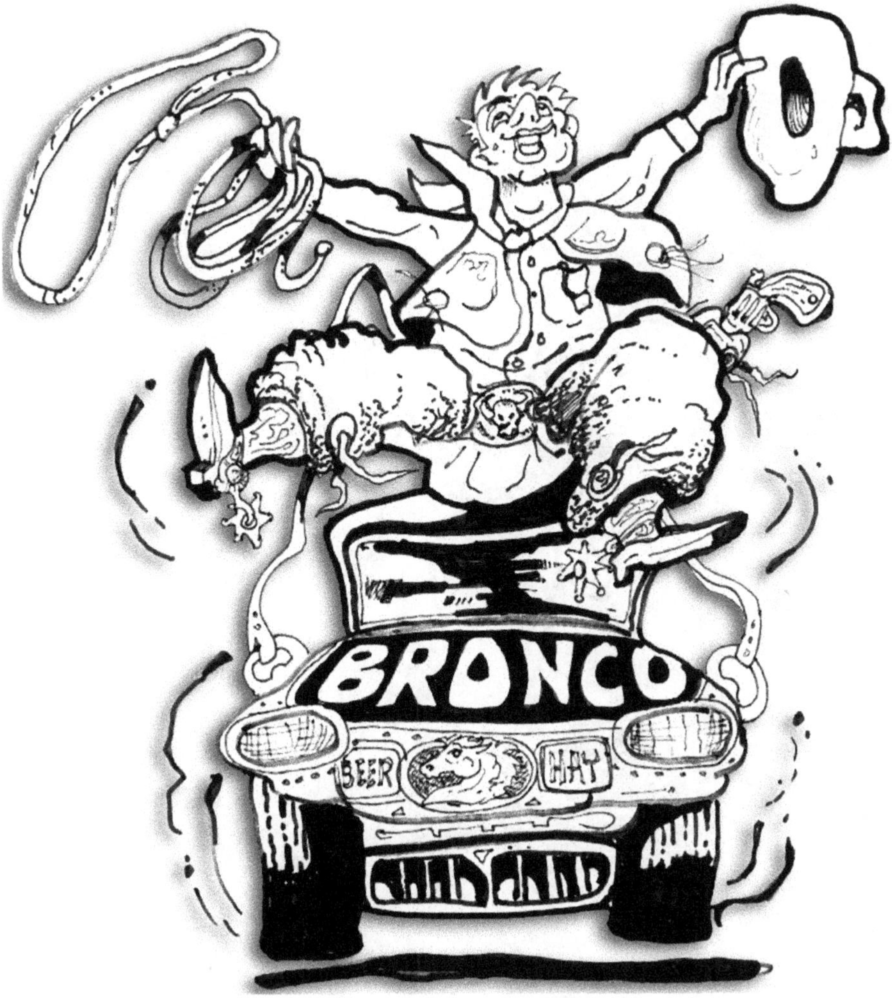
BRONCO
BEER
HAY

Ridin' the "Steel Horse".

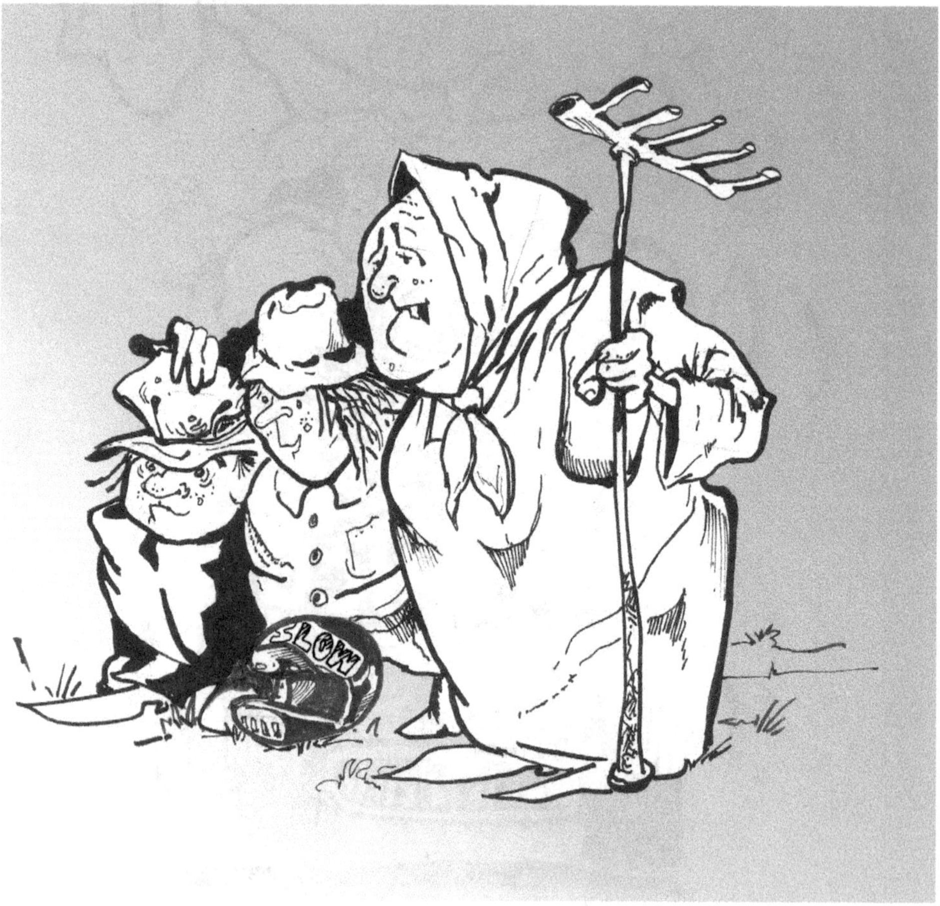
SLOW

NASCAR future drivers

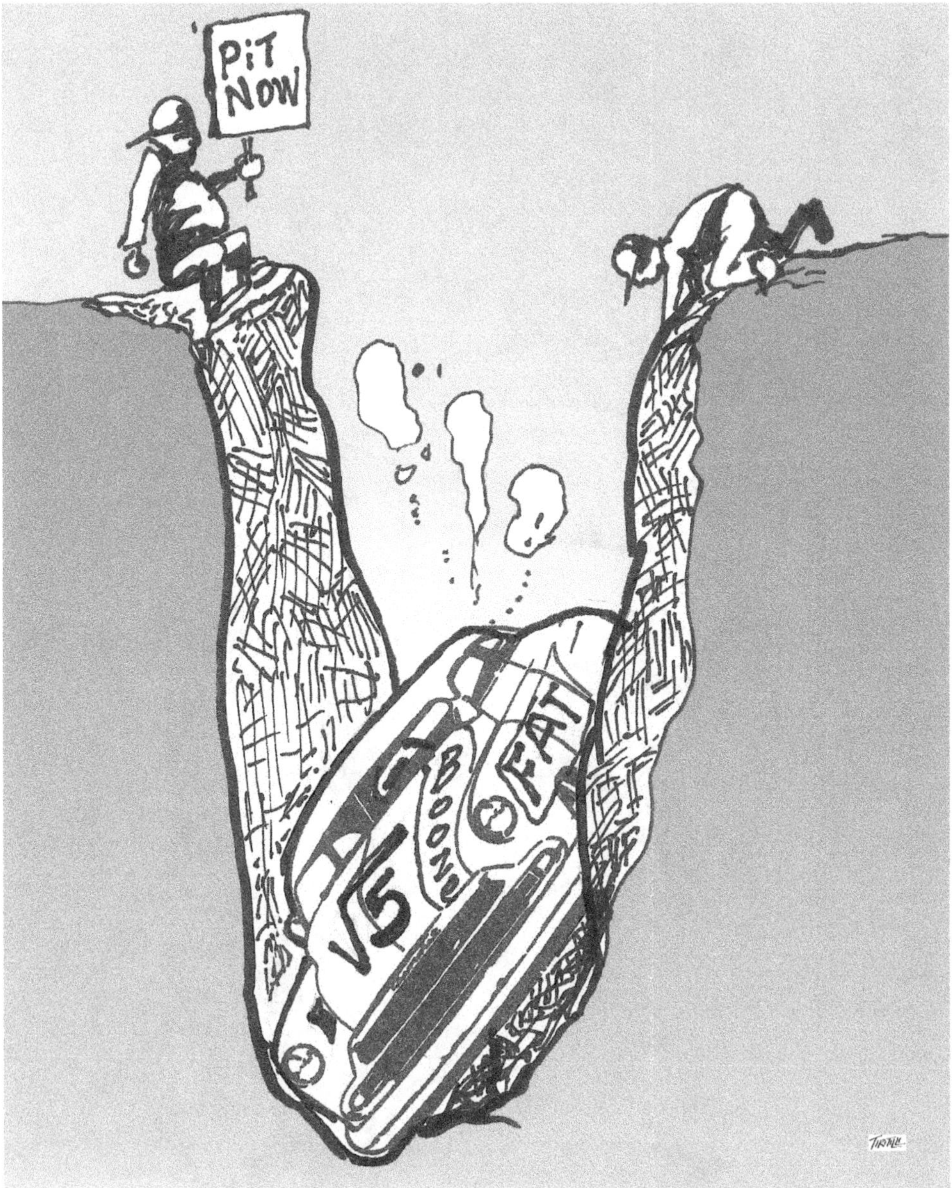
PIT NOW
FAT
BOONE
V5

Wrong Pit

SHE's a race car

Raceitis

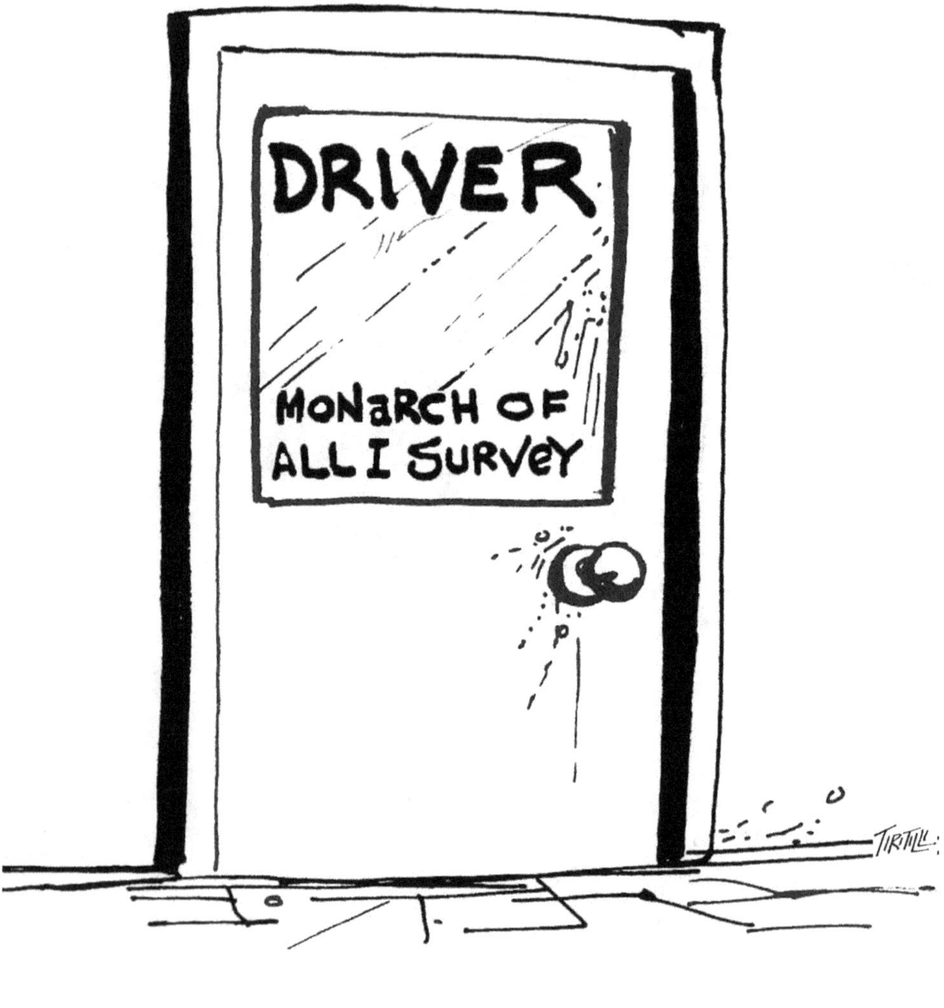
DRIVER
MONARCH OF ALL I SURVEY
TIRITILLI

"Are you going to *"retire"* me?"

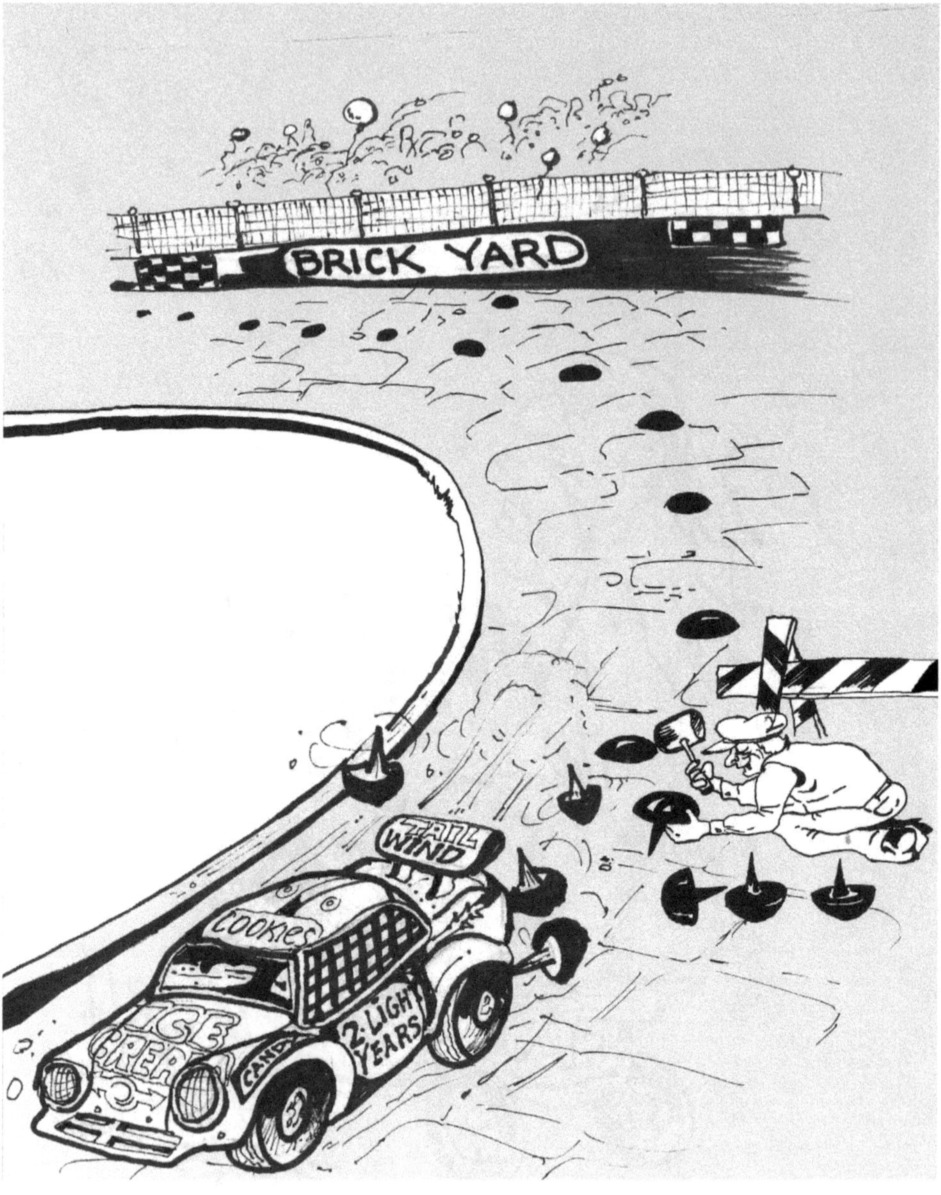
BRICK YARD
TAIL WIND
COOKIES
2 LIGHT YEARS
ICE CREAM
CANDY

Speed bumps?

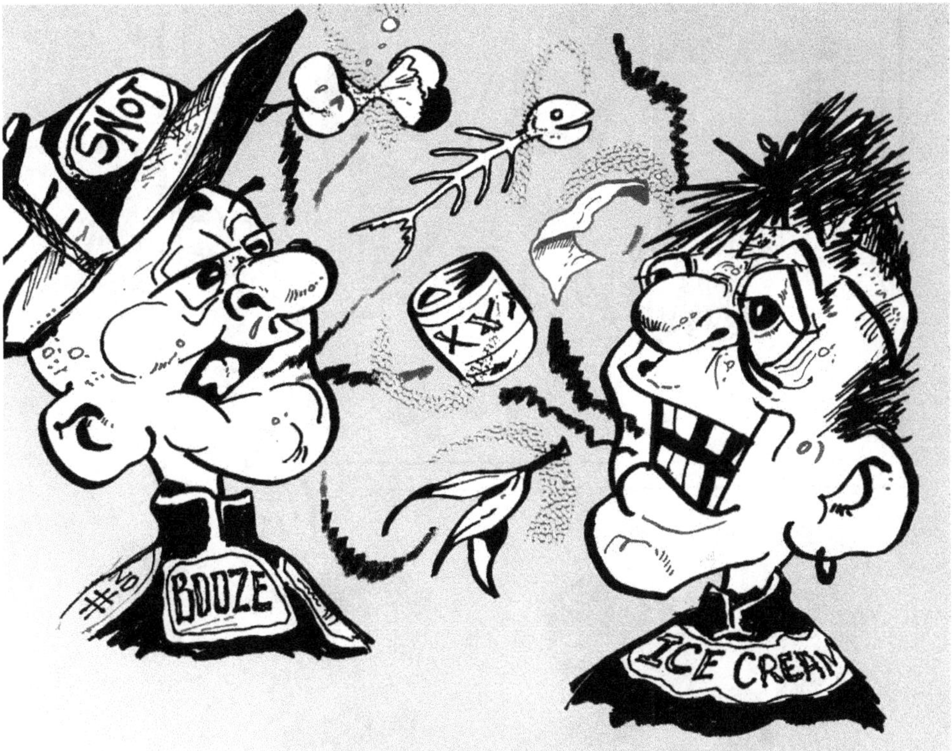
SNOT
BOOZE
ICE CREAM

Auto Racing TRASH TALK

Beginning FanAuto School

Abraham Lincoln invents first race car.

www.ingramcontent.com/pod-product-compliance
Lightning Source LLC
Chambersburg PA
CBHW060646030426
42337CB00018B/3478